W9-BIQ-596

Date: 6/27/17

J 741.5973 PER
Perkins, Chloe,
The great American story of
Charlie Brown, Snoopy, a...

PALM BEACH COUNTY
LIBRARY SYSTEM
3650 SUMMIT BLVD.
WEST PALM BEACH. FL 33406

HISTORY OF FUN STUFF

The Great American Story of Charlie Brown, Snoopy, and the Peanuts Gang!

by Chloe Perkins
illustrated by Scott Burroughs
featuring artwork by Charles M. Schulz

Ready-to-Read

Simon Spotlight
New York   London   Toronto   Sydney   New Delhi

SIMON SPOTLIGHT
An imprint of Simon & Schuster Children's Publishing Division
1230 Avenue of the Americas, New York, New York 10020
This Simon Spotlight edition May 2017
© 2017 Peanuts Worldwide LLC
All rights reserved, including the right of reproduction in whole or in part in any form.
SIMON SPOTLIGHT, READY-TO-READ, and colophon are registered trademarks of
Simon & Schuster, Inc.
For information about special discounts for bulk purchases, please contact Simon & Schuster Special Sales
at 1-866-506-1949 or business@simonandschuster.com.
Manufactured in the United States of America 0417 LAK
2 4 6 8 10 9 7 5 3 1
Library of Congress Cataloging-in-Publication Data
Names: Perkins, Chloe, author. | Burroughs, Scott, illustrator. | Schulz, Charles M. (Charles Monroe),
1922–2000, artist. Title: The great American story of Charlie Brown, Snoopy, and the Peanuts gang! / by
Chloe Perkins ; illustrated by Scott Burroughs ; featuring artwork by Charles M. Schulz. Description:
New York : Simon Spotlight, 2017. | Series: History of fun stuff | Series: Ready-to-read. Level three
Identifiers: LCCN 2017006367 (print) | LCCN 2017006746 (ebook) | ISBN 9781481495530 (paperback)|
ISBN 9781481495547 (hardcover) | ISBN 9781481495554 (eBook) Subjects: LCSH: Schulz, Charles M.
(Charles Monroe), 1922–2000. Peanuts—Juvenile literature. | Comic books, strips, etc.—United States—
History and criticism—Juvenile literature. | BISAC: JUVENILE NONFICTION / Readers / Beginner. |
JUVENILE NONFICTION / Comics & Graphic Novels / History. | JUVENILE NONFICTION / Media
Tie-In. Classification: LCC PN6728.P4 P47 2017 (print) | LCC PN6728.P4 (eBook) | DDC 741.5/973—dc23
LC record available at https://lccn.loc.gov/2017006367

CONTENTS

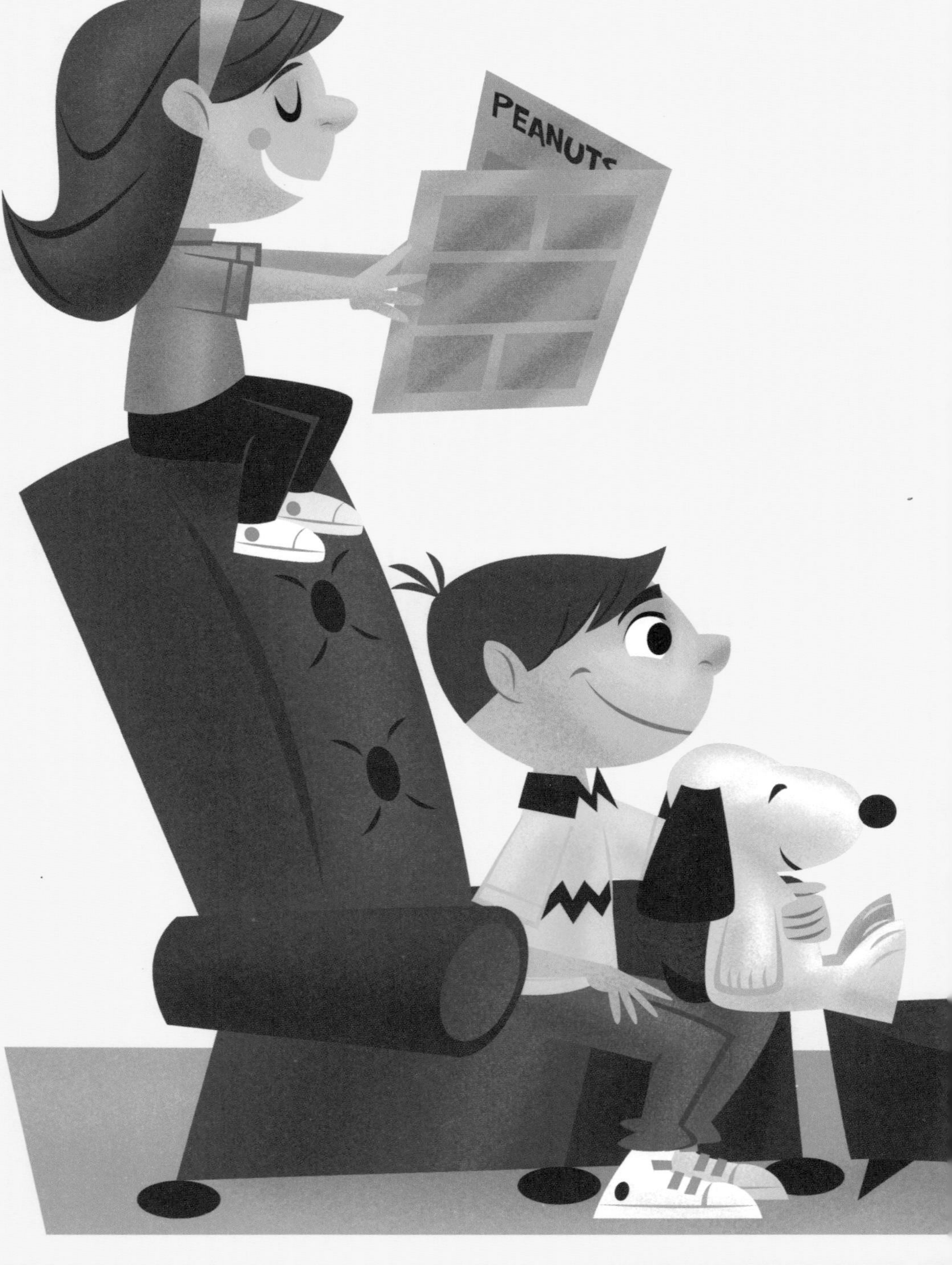
PEANUTS

CHAPTER 1
Who Was Charles M. Schulz?

Everyone has heard of Charlie Brown and Snoopy. Maybe you've seen *The Peanuts Movie* or read the Peanuts comic strip in the newspaper. Maybe you and your family watch *It's the Great Pumpkin, Charlie Brown* every year around Halloween, or you've had a stuffed Snoopy since you were little.

But do you know where Charlie Brown, Snoopy, and the Peanuts gang came from? Or how the first Peanuts cartoon came to be? Or how Snoopy became the first beagle in space?

Well, wonder no more! By the end of this book you'll know everything there is to know about the artist behind these characters, Charles M. Schulz, and his incredible comic strip. You'll be a History of Fun Stuff Expert on Charlie Brown, Snoopy, and the Peanuts gang!

7

It all began in Minneapolis, Minnesota, in 1922, when Charles Monroe Schulz was born. His dad, Carl, was a barber, and his mom, Dena, was a homemaker. Charles's uncle nicknamed him "Sparky" after a character in a comic strip, and it seemed he was fated for a career in comics. From childhood through old age, everyone who knew Charles called him Sparky.

As a kid, Charles loved drawing and reading comic strips in the newspaper. He would sketch characters like Popeye and the Three Little Pigs on the covers of his classmates' notebooks.

Charles's love of drawing continued into his teen years. When he was fourteen, Charles published his first cartoon. The Schulzes' family dog, Spike, had a habit of eating strange objects—even things that weren't very good for him, like pins and tacks! Spike's appetite gave Charles a chance to see what it was like to be a cartoonist when his local newspaper printed a sketch he'd drawn of Spike, in the *Ripley's Believe It or Not!* comic strip.

During Charles's senior year of high school, Dena saw an advertisement for a cartooning course with Federal Schools (later known as Art Instruction Schools). People could mail in their drawings and receive feedback from real artists. Charles wanted to take the class, but the course was expensive. Carl didn't mind the cost; he wanted to help his son hone his talent. Charles enrolled in the course and graduated from high school the following year in 1940.

Charles continued drawing and learning from his cartooning course after high school. Around this time, though, Charles's mother became sick. Charles and his dad cared for Dena, but a few years later Charles was drafted into the army during World War II.

Dena was still very sick, and the doctors said she might pass away before Charles would return from service. Before he left, Dena told her son that if the family got another dog, they should name him Snoopy. Dena passed away later that year.

In 1945, after Charles was discharged from the army, he began teaching for Art Instruction Schools, the same program that had helped him improve his cartooning skills. He continued to submit his artwork to newspapers in hopes of one day publishing a comic strip (also known as a panel cartoon) of his own. Two of Charles's comics were published in the *Topix* comic book in February and April of 1947. Still, Charles wanted to write a weekly strip, and in June of 1947, his wish came true!

CHAPTER 2
Peanuts Conquers the World
(and Space, Too!)

Li'l Folks was Charles's first weekly panel cartoon. It was about kids, but it made both children and adults laugh. It was first published in the *St. Paul Pioneer Press* in June 1947.

Charles wanted his comic strip to have a wider reach. He started submitting to syndicates, companies that could publish *Li'l Folks* in newspapers across the country. After many rejections, he finally received a contract with United Feature Syndicate in 1950.

But there was a catch. United Features
Syndicate already had another comic strip
by Tack Knight called *Little Folks*. They
suggested Charles rename his comic
strip *Peanuts*. Charles disagreed—he
felt the name made the cartoon sound
like it wasn't important—but the name
stuck. The first Peanuts comic strip was
published on October 2, 1950.

Readers loved Peanuts. They found Charlie Brown, Snoopy, and the gang's adventures to be both funny and wise. Parents and children around the country could read the comic strip together.

By 1952, forty newspapers ran the comic. By 1958, three hundred and fifty-five newspapers printed it! Forty more newspapers outside of the United States ran the comic as well. Things were looking up for Charlie Brown!

Over time, companies saw how much the public loved Peanuts, and so they began making Peanuts toys, books, and more! In 1955, the camera company Kodak featured the Peanuts characters in a handbook. In 1958, Hungerford Plastics created figurines of Charlie Brown, Snoopy, Linus, and Lucy. Hallmark, a major greeting card company, made the first Peanuts greeting cards in 1960.

Then, in 1962, Charles published *Happiness Is a Warm Puppy,* the first Peanuts book to feature his characters outside of a comic strip, and incredible sales skyrocketed it onto the *New York Times* bestseller list. But the success didn't stop there!

During this time, the Peanuts gang was animated for the first time. In 1959, Charles worked with animator Bill Melendez to bring his characters to life in a popular commercial for the Ford Motor Company. In the ad, Linus, Charlie Brown, and Lucy ask about the company's most popular car, the Ford Falcon.

Throughout the 1950s and 1960s, Charles won many awards and honors for Peanuts. He received two Reuben Awards from the National Cartoonists Society in 1955 and 1964, becoming the first person ever to win the award twice. Yale University named Charles "Humorist of the Year" in 1958, and Peanuts was named "Best Humor Strip of the Year" by the National Cartoonists Society in 1962. To top it all off, Peanuts was featured on the cover of *TIME* magazine in 1965.

CHAPTER 3
Peanuts on TV

As you can see, by the mid-1960s, Peanuts had become a worldwide hit. Lee Mendelson, a TV producer, wanted to make a documentary about the comic strip. He visited Charles, and they agreed to do a half-hour special with a few minutes of animation. Charles contacted Bill Melendez, who had created the animation for the Ford Falcon commercial. Composer and jazz musician Vince Guaraldi even created original music for the documentary, a now famous song called "Linus and Lucy." Have you ever heard the song?

Even though Peanuts was very popular at the time, many TV networks didn't want to broadcast the documentary. They weren't sure it was something viewers would be interested in.

A few years passed, and just when Lee and Charles were about to give up hope, the Coca-Cola Company stepped in!

Coca-Cola wanted to sponsor a special program for the holiday season. They thought a Peanuts Christmas cartoon would be a hit.

Charles and Lee had to prepare an outline of the story quickly—in just a few days! They presented it to the company and were approved to start production. Charles worked on the script, while Bill drew the animation in storyboards. Storyboards are a series of illustrations artists draw to help visualize how a final piece of animation will look.

Once the script was in place and the storyboards were under way, it was time to cast actors to be the voices of Charlie Brown, Linus, Lucy, and the rest. At the time, most cartoon characters were voiced by adults, but Charles felt strongly that his characters should be voiced by real kids. While most of the main characters were voiced by child actors, other background voices were done by kids from Bill's neighborhood!

The youngest in the cast (who voiced Sally) was six years old, and since she hadn't learned how to read yet, the lines had to be recited to her. Bill voiced Snoopy, speeding up recordings of himself talking to make his voice sound different.

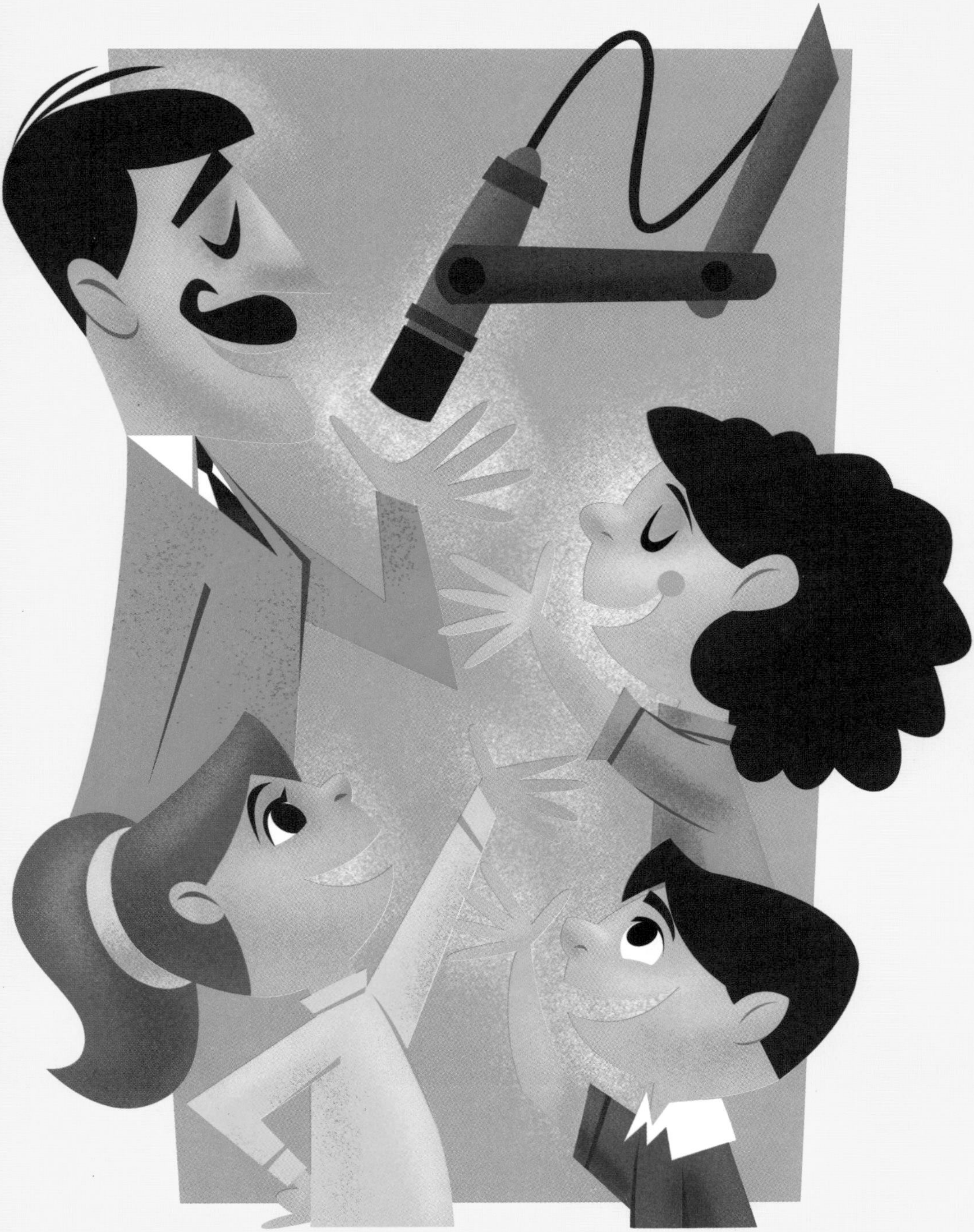

The TV network CBS had provided the money Charles, Bill, and Lee needed to create *A Charlie Brown Christmas*. But when they showed CBS executives the finished movie, the executives didn't like it.

Luckily for us, CBS still broadcast it. *A Charlie Brown Christmas* debuted on December 9, 1965, and it was an instant hit—more than fifteen million viewers tuned in! The special went on to win a Peabody Award and an Emmy Award for outstanding children's programming.

Aside from all the awards, what really made *A Charlie Brown Christmas* important was that it kick-started many, many more animated features for Peanuts. Some forty-five TV specials have since been created, along with five movies! Charles, Bill, and Lee continued working

on these specials together, and Vince composed even more music for the cartoons. A stage musical, *You're a Good Man, Charlie Brown*, opened in 1967 and has since become one of the most produced musicals in the US. Peanuts was here to stay!

There was still one place that Peanuts had never gone before—outer space. That all changed in 1968, when Snoopy became an astrobeagle and NASA's "watchdog" for flight safety. When the Apollo 10 rocket launched in May of 1969, astronauts Gene Cernan, John Young, and Thomas Stafford traveled all the way around the moon and back with two spacecraft. *Snoopy* was the name of the lunar module (a part of the spacecraft that would separate and land on the moon) and *Charlie Brown* was the name of the command module (the part of the spacecraft where the crew operated). That's one small step for beagles, one giant leap for Peanuts-kind!

CHAPTER 4
The Legacy of Peanuts

By 1975, its twenty-fifth anniversary, the Peanuts comic strip was carried in 1,480 newspapers in the United States and 175 foreign newspapers around the world—with an estimated ninety million readers! The comic strip had achieved success beyond Charles's imagination, and he continued to draw new Peanuts comic strips every day.

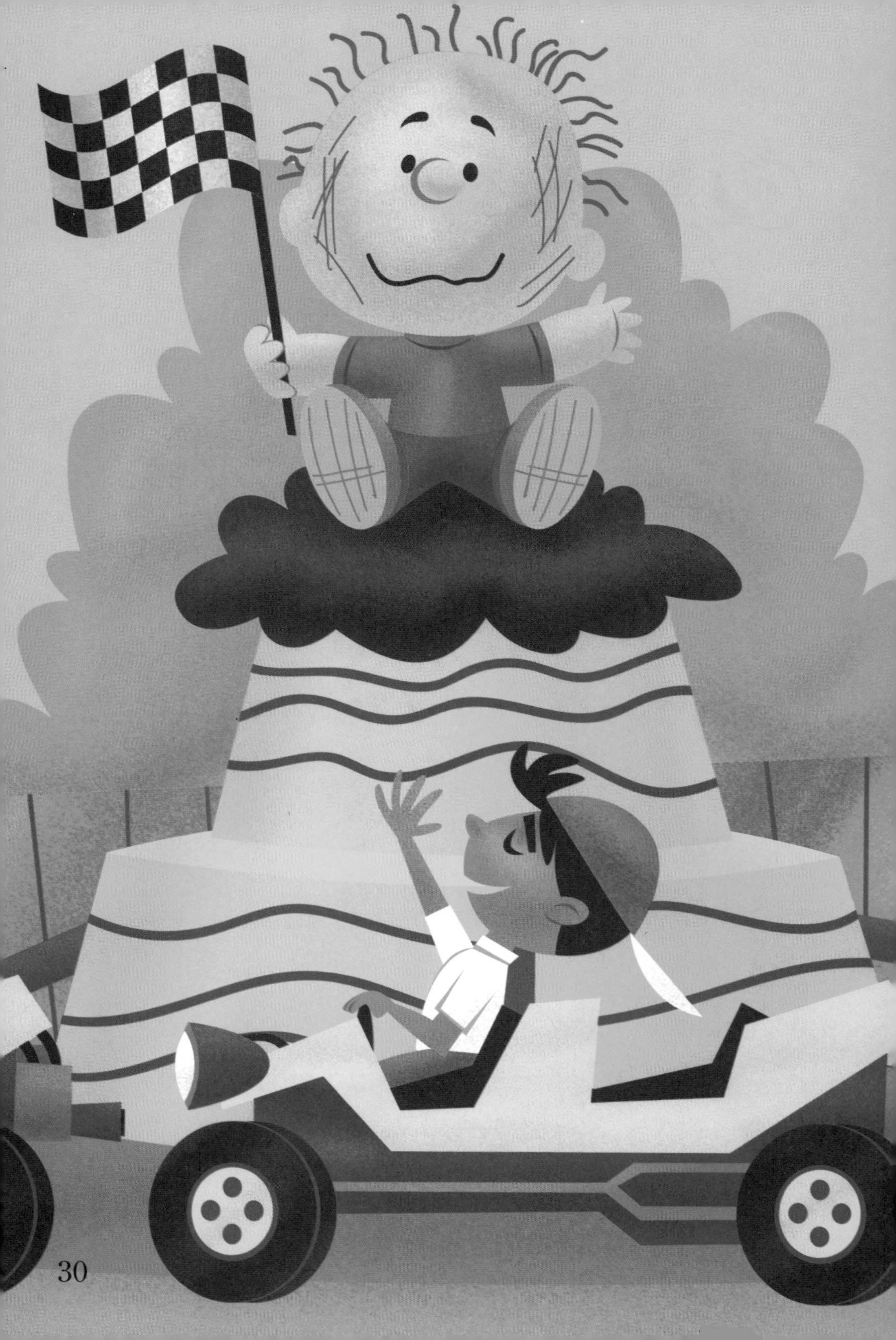

As time went on, more people wanted a piece of Peanuts for themselves. Books, stuffed animals, toys, and games were created alongside the continuing comic strip.

In 1983, Knott's Berry Farm, an amusement park in California, opened Camp Snoopy, a section of the park dedicated to kids under twelve. Camp Snoopy was the first such amusement park specifically for young kids.

Charles became one of the most celebrated cartoonists of all time. He was inducted into the Cartoonist Hall of Fame by the Museum of Cartoon Art in 1986.

The French government named Charles a Commander of Arts and Letters in 1990, and he was awarded the Order of Merit from the Italian Minister of Culture in 1992.

Charles even received a star on the
Hollywood Walk of Fame in 1996.

Charles announced his retirement on December 14, 1999, because of health problems. By this point, the comic strip was appearing in more than 2,600 newspapers worldwide.

On February 12, 2000, Charles died at the age of seventy-seven. On the following day, declared "Charles M. Schulz Day" by California lawmakers, the final Peanuts comic strip appeared in newspapers.

Charles received many more honors even after he passed away, including the Congressional Gold Medal, one of the highest civilian awards given by the United States government.

Even though Charles M. Schulz is gone, Peanuts lives on! The Peanuts comic strips that Charles created still appear in newspapers across the country, and even more Peanuts cartoons, short films, and movies are being made. Parents and kids are still finding Charlie Brown's and Snoopy's adventures just as funny and wise as their grandparents did sixty years ago.

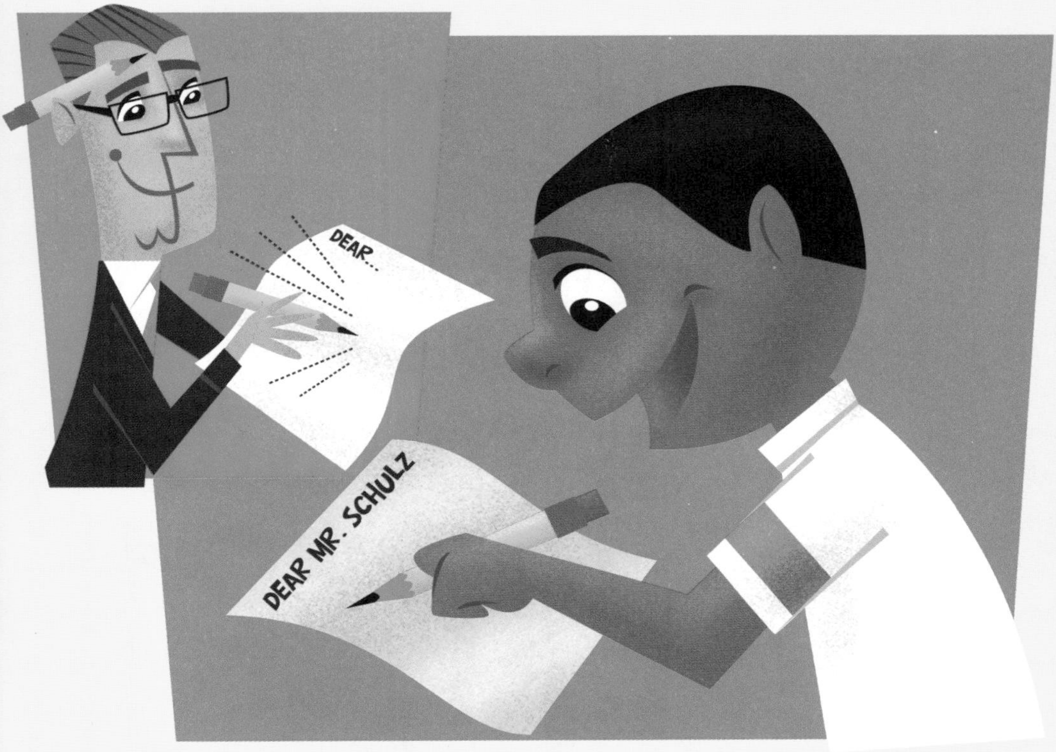
DEAR
DEAR MR. SCHULZ

Perhaps most important, Charles M. Schulz has influenced millions of people, including famous artists such as Bill Watterson, creator of the comic strip *Calvin and Hobbes*. When Watterson was in the fourth grade, he wrote a fan letter to Charles, and to his shock, Charles responded with words of encouragement. “In countless ways,” Watterson said, “Schulz blazed the wide trail that most every cartoonist since has tried to follow.”

EXPERT

HISTORY
OF FUN STUFF
EXPERT
ON
CHARLIE BROWN,
SNOOPY, AND THE
PEANUTS GANG

Congratulations! You've come to the end of this book. You are now an official History of Fun Stuff Expert on Charlie Brown, Snoopy, and the Peanuts gang. Go ahead and impress your friends and family with all the cool stuff you've learned. And remember the incredible stories behind the characters next time you see a Peanuts cartoon or read a Peanuts comic strip!

Hey, kids! Now that you're an expert on the history of Charlie Brown, Snoopy, and the Peanuts gang, turn the page to learn even more about the comic, and some art, science, and geography along the way!

How to Draw Charlie Brown!

Many artists train for years to draw the Peanuts characters just right, and trust us, it's no walk in the park! Do you think you have what it takes? Read the instructions below to learn how to draw Charlie Brown!

Draw a big circle, but leave the middle right part of your circle open.

In the opening of your big circle, draw a small half circle for Charlie Brown's ear. On the left side of the big circle, add another small sliver of a circle for Charlie Brown's other ear.

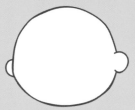

Next, in the middle of the big circle, draw another small half circle, a little bigger than the ears. This is Charlie Brown's nose! Draw a little dot on either side of the nose for his eyes.

Then you add the hair. Charlie Brown's hair looks like a sideways three with a loop in the middle.

And finally, to draw Charlie Brown's smile, draw an arc going from the bottom of Charlie Brown's left ear to the bottom of Charlie Brown's right ear. To get the curve right, match the curve you already made in the shape of Charlie Brown's face.

Science of Animation

Did you know that when you watch a cartoon, it's actually tricking your brain? It's true!

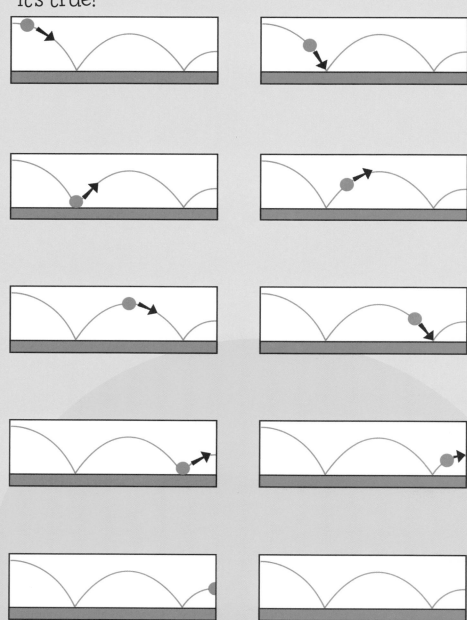

We see movement in a cartoon because animators have created many individual drawings, called frames, that simulate motion. Each frame is slightly different than the frame that came before it. For example, if you were going to animate a bouncing ball, each frame would show the ball bouncing a little bit higher than the frame before it.

In the early days of animation, each frame had to be drawn by hand. Today, most animators use computers to help illustrate the frames.

Once the frames are completed, a projector or computer program shows the frames very quickly; usually twenty-four frames are shown every second! Our brain sees all these frames together as movement because of **persistence of vision** and the **phi phenomenon**.

Persistence of vision happens because your brain keeps an image of what you see for a fraction of a second longer than you actually see it.

The phi phenomenon happens when you are shown still images very quickly. Even though the images themselves aren't moving, your brain fills in the gaps between each image and sees it as motion.

When you put these two things together, it causes you to see movement, even though you're really only seeing a bunch of still images really quickly! Pretty neat trick, right?

1   2   3   4

The Geography of Peanuts

We have one more fun fact for you about Peanuts: Many of the places that Snoopy visits in Peanuts comic strips are real! Charles was inspired by many places he lived in, visited, and read about throughout his life. Have you been to any of these places?

Point Lobos, California

In a series of comic strips, Snoopy and the Beagle Scouts go on a photo hike to Point Lobos, and two of the Beagle Scouts (Bill and Harriet) later get married there! Point Lobos State Natural Reserve is a beautiful park right on the Pacific Ocean. It has many hiking trails and is home to animals such as harbor seals, cormorants, and whales.

POINT LOBOS

CALIFORNIA

Verdun, France

As the World War I Flying Ace, Snoopy often talks about going to Verdun to fight the Red Baron. Verdun is a small city in northeastern France, and it was the site of a real battle—the longest and biggest battle of World War I, the Battle of Verdun. Memorials and monuments for the battle can be found throughout the city.

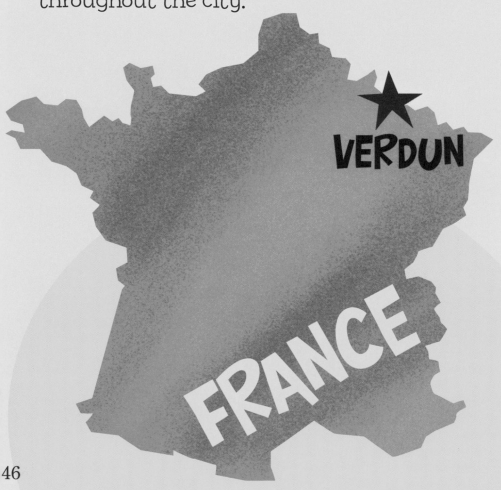

VERDUN

FRANCE

Needles, California

Snoopy's brother, Spike, lives in the desert outside of Needles, California, but did you know that it's a real place, too? Charles and his family lived in the town of Needles from 1928 to 1930.

CALIFORNIA

NEEDLE

Being an expert on something means you can get an awesome score on a quiz on that subject! Take this

HISTORY OF CHARLIE BROWN, SNOOPY, AND THE PEANUTS GANG QUIZ

to see how much you've learned.

1. What year was Charles M. Schulz born?
   a. 1922   b. 1622   c. 2010

2. What did Charles M. Schulz draw in his first published artwork?
   a. a boat   b. a house   c. his family dog

3. Why did Charles M. Schulz have to change the name of his comic strip to Peanuts?
   a. No one liked it. b. He was hungry.   c. Another comic strip had a
                                                similar name.

4. Who animated Peanuts for the first time?
   a. Bill Melendez   b. Lee Mendelson   c. Charles M. Schulz

5. Charles M. Schulz was the first artist to win which award twice?
   a. Academy Award   b. Reuben Award   c. Nobel Prize

6. Which company sponsored *A Charlie Brown Christmas*?
   a. Coca-Cola   b. Nestle   c. Hershey

7. By 1975, Peanuts had how many readers worldwide?
   a. ten   b. thirty thousand   c. ninety million

8. Camp Snoopy is part of what theme park?
   a. Disneyland   b. Knott's Berry Farm c. Sea World

Answers: 1. a 2. c 3. c 4. a 5. b 6. a 7. c 8. b

REPRODUCIBLE